NO MATTER THE LATITUDE, DEAREST SKY,

AHSAHTA PRESS

BOISE, IDAHO
2013

THE NEW SERIES
#52

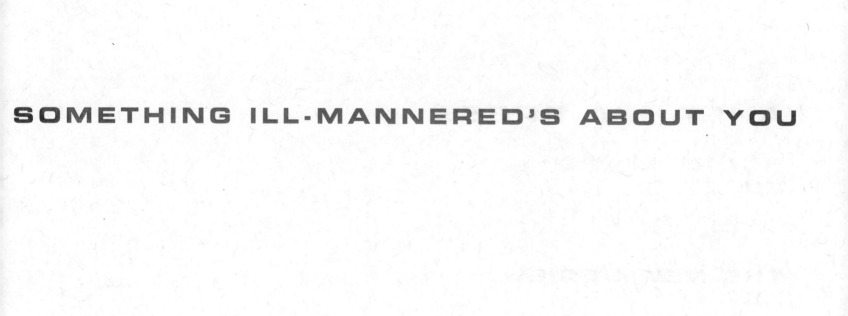

SOMETHING ILL-MANNERED'S ABOUT YOU

CLOUD VS. CLOUD

ETHAN PAQUIN

Ahsahta Press, Boise State University, Boise, Idaho 83725-1525
ahsahtapress.org
Cover design by Quemadura
Book design by Janet Holmes
Printed in Canada

LIBRARY OF CONGRESS CATALOGING-IN-PUBLICATION DATA

PAQUIN, ETHAN.
[POEMS. SELECTIONS]
CLOUD VS. CLOUD / ETHAN PAQUIN.
PAGES CM. -- (THE NEW SERIES ; #52)
INCLUDES BIBLIOGRAPHICAL REFERENCES.
POEMS.
ISBN 978-1-934103-38-8 (PAPERBACK : ALK. PAPER) — ISBN 1-934103-38-1 (PAPERBACK : ALK. PAPER)
I. TITLE.
PS3566.A6235C56 2013
2012043062

ACKNOWLEDGMENTS

Some of the poems herein first appeared in journals: *Big Bell:* "Chapter," "Insufficiency," "Pisces"; *Cutbank:* "Self-Portrait," "Songeur"; *Damn the Caesars:* "Intellectual Stanzae," "Life Imitates Cento"; *Eleven Eleven:* "Ars Nihil," "Interrupted Narrative: Marienbad," "Lumpen District"; *The Laurel Review:* "Kinoglaz," "Thirty-Nine Threads"; *MiPOesias* (online): "About a Wall," "Silent Morning," "Tarn Star Lake"; *Origin:* "Green Green Hill," "O Holy Hill," "The Lot Drawn"; *Parthenon West Review:* "Exeunt"; *Pleiades:* "a la Plage," "Disjunctive Field [Artillary]," "Dark Ballad of the 73rd Page"; *Verse,* "Neige [Three Scenes]." Some also appeared in the chapbook *Nineains* (Hand Held Editions, 2009).

CONTENTS

ENDEARMENT

PATRON SAINT GUNPOWDER

ENDEARMENT

SELF-PORTRAIT

This was the last poem I ever wrote.
It came to me under the blue sky,
under the bluest sky. Do you know
blue? Have you ever seen a blue settle
against the rest of the universe so
starkly, or bury itself so deeply into
you that it made you think of a spring
cutting through the ancient gray rock
of your favourite childhood hillside?
Do you remember childhood? The
rabbits in your grandfather's coop,
the sway of your uncle's boat atop
the cool Atlantic inlet, the long brown
hair of your mother in a photo you
didn't quite fathom upon glancing it
at age six, the first your father shaved
off his moustache, the first taste of berry
from your grandmother's pie, the calm in
your aunt's eyes as she led you onward
through a gallery of American paintings,
the sadness in your brother's young eyes
as he awaited some unknown in the attic
as he played with a fragile china tea set,

the first time you noticed a flag flutter
and realized the wind is older than all,
the first time you cared to notice the sun
setting over the former pastures, once
fertile cow pastures and thence plots
for the dull lives of condominium dwellers,
the trails cut in the woods and the poison
ivy and oak, the nail clean through the foot
and the first knowledge of damage? Do you?
Do you think anything is as awful as purple
after the rains? I remember the first thunder-
storm—I was there, and I wasn't afraid, but
I felt it was terrible, I felt punishment, I felt
chased, as on the high mountaintop in the west
of the central region of my home state when,
after summiting, the clamour and fearful crack
descended atop me. I remember words coming
in much the same way, and now after years of
plying them, I feel no better or better off than
I ever was before, and perhaps even sadder.
I remember saying *je t'aime* to a young girl
I'd go on to marry, and upon whom my fear
and irrationality and hate would be heaped,
I remember the first time she took me in
her mouth, I remember a smile she hasn't had
in many years. I remember my son the second
he was born, for I was the first to hold him and

he looked at me as if he had known me forever,
that he had known me before and would always.
I was told to not write a poem about this moment
for the moment was the poem, but here, eight years
later, I feel I must write it for I see him get taller
and I see my hair thinning and every day, though
surrounded by friends, I sense what a shoal far out
in the Atlantic must sense when it is countenanced
by the evilest black that the hurricane-swept eastern
sky can offer up. I see the kindest black in the eyes
of my daughter, who frolics as if she has already
danced in some far-off France or Greece, happy
as the glint of sun in the dry hills of her ancestry.
I look at the clutter on my desk, worthless clutter,
and then to the books upon my shelves I never
thought I'd actually read, and now they are all
mostly read. I miss the mountains, I miss the ocean,
and sometimes both places seem to compete for me
so that I feel as if I'm being unfaithful to one or
the other. I miss the sleeping on a February slope
high atop Mount Flume, going to bed at 3 p.m. for
the sun was already dying out, and huddling against
even the snow neath my sleeping bag for comfort.
Do you remember things like these? If I speak of
such things, you know. You have as many moments
as I—they are numerous, like the branches or cones
of the northern forest. In the deep recesses of such,

one will find creatures if one tries hard enough, and
sometimes the looks on their faces are tragic. Do you
want to make amends with them, as I do, for leveling
their homes, or for writing so insipidly about them?
Do you wish you'd catalogued every berry you'd picked,
from the very first at age three in a rural orchard whose
wind-socks flittered in a light June, or every autumn apple
you'd seen fallen into decay? When the dawn is imminent,
do you find yourself counting the thousands of hours
you've got left? The dozens of hours a loved one has left?
The unknowable length of time has left a marriage, one
so strip-mined and soured you lose all hope in forgiveness
of self? The great distance between where a shell washes
upon the beach and where it might have wanted to land?
And all this while, the questions keep getting posed and
the slow descent makes our baskets unsteady and eyes
affix upon some point of arrival that makes this last poem
and its writing superfluous and trite, not nearly as permanent
as the waft of the anonymous hawks above the mountains
and the fact the birds are unburdened by all these things.

FIRST POEM

To be every sound and no sound at once
Is the movie theatre on christmas afternoon—
Is the lode of the wilderness breeze—
Is the omniscient narrator of our novels—
Is the barrenness of prayer and orgasm—
Is the summit of some peak, say,
found in the upper Appalachians—
Is the face of cloud over cloud—
Is the expression of one's mother—
Is the i actually became my father—
Is the concept of property—
Is bloodline is attic—
Is lover is arc—
Is traicere is outsill—
Is meadow is hinge—
Is our greatest familiarity—
Is our terrain most aweful—

WINTER COUNTRY LOT

clack of bough on a cascade depressed
and kicking back, eight million birds

away, resounds in an ungrafted stump,
life long since peter'd away, incarnation

as birch long tossed in a universe gray
floating off—memory's flotsam. dead

cherries, slow, icy slough of february's
underboot mud—here are the prettiest

things in the current winter catalog;
ochre's in, carrot-green and slate, too,

and dapple they a wide slope. across its
slow'd timbre, no planet resounds at all

ABOUT A WALL

about   a wall
is   its optimal
wallness   it

will inter   as
a forest   the eyes
of   summer animals

*

day   of sixty degrees
  brack   or sun   take
your pick   it's about

seeing   past a red, brick,
painted-over,   wall [&] beyond
you,   young woman

THE LOT DRAWN

Sorry, artists, meadow's been reserved—
and so's the corner of the lot in which
a woman sees her breasts in clips of sun
all tinged with dearth. You know that blue out there?

It's the blue of property, you know,
the blue no painter's ever gotten down,
the blue no painter's ever gotten out
from in his eyes. As such, you must move on.

GREEN GREEN HILL

for you a green green hill that stretches up and up
there what is found is nothing like anything anybody
else has ever discovered.   nothing like a vacuous summer
of empty darkness   here   take my high plain, prairie
or plateau   intervale in which birches sway lightly

+

i never knew this person before   indeed she   like all
others   has wandered   and her frock has billowd
her hair   's brown as a meandering Oregon coast.
stark and brown   the birds flought from a high   hill
about death   but this is not the place nor the time.

+

our times end too quickly   time a ribbon must sever
for you a lace ribbon for your hair brown   brown,
for your hair, brown,   this dream   and each man
will linger by the side of a snowy road and   then
will he stare out into the woods   his breath the thing

+

the stone wall laid by gone hands the thing   the air
the flake clung to his shoulder jacket   then there
through boughs a glint of sun   that is the thing
that will keep him in that spot looking for meaning.
and there is nothing wildly difficult about that

+

this daffodil hill i would leave on my door   for you
, someone worthy of daffodils.   perhaps may you
instead want a special breaker   upon the water of a sea
carved from stone only   for you   perhaps to you the lap
of sea-water is as pleasing as the language of France.

+

what is known, nothing   what has come before, ever
anything   and what do we want, nothing that can be
articulated. the birches, are they gentle?, and will you
walk there sometime?   i want to see you walk toward
the slope and then turn to me   that is want   is what

SONNET

there there played a sun ballad long-cast cliff face
basked in there's heat and thus the ceiling which's
thirty-hundred-thousand breaths of birds away
in an ether lichening bluish due to contamine of
love that swept her blush gracing her cheeks and
her posture behoovéd a young woman disrobing
to a view of grackles or pine-top green thistles all
these minions and colours in this our waterhouse
universe of a new low and vaprous pond a pond hers
a place for her to sit, simply. there she could may-
pole around language, this lovely daughter of poetry
displaced by difficulty by the new spheric's mesmerist
the playful man the lover of language and of beasts and
and the way of hair of beautiful redheads in the woods

~~

so you come writing to me and you're expecting what
exactly but some kind of poem and therein some kind
of genius, is that it?, well, i've not been in love since
since decade relapsed into arcade since you saw la mer
since outré and since bouffant and the death of musics
as the death of pine needles they all they all go somewhere

don't they?, and lust is what drives a poem and not love.
there is no secret i don't know—i heard myself calling
in a tirade and then it was or was it the poem? and off
i went thenceforth to a lack of rhyme to the vers libre
con livres for the trees unto themselves are locked for
certain a tree is an upright energy but never outward
and no neither can the page spring to anything but no
life at all save its monochrome intangibility it's all here

~~

i want to be in the Corser with Marc i want to be in Boston
with Walker i want to be on Mount Bond i am still there
i want to be with my friends on the dodged and burned
known as the landing strip for a beaucoup of tiny planes
lightly wafting to earth after some happenstance partigua.
i want to know what i meant by a word in a thirty-year-old
woman's eyes as it backflipped and irradiated her brains in
the café that one evening i can barely recall i was so drunk
on the idea that i needed to be in love with being intelligible
but no one knows their own arms, even, so how can we know
what we say is a vessel that can actually my i's are lowercase
i will not affirm myself she finally died was screaming in pain
and some were relieved to see her at the vale someone else
o lord are you indeed benign, do you indeed hear i screaming

~~

there there my little student there is always a raindrop for you
my my little student did you not master that pentametric well
there there there it is you're going to miss it say sir do you die
when on command their cotton drop dendritic malifestations
like watermelons in on a display cart case on in submarketplace
la Marais las meniges the virtues of the fruit skin and her eyes
all of which partook of a sun hidden by a villanelle carnival my
my dear student i don't know why the holly on the head groweth
so we need study it slowly, as a roaming bardesse and her song
do filleth an aire dearly bereft of my fact that the oceanic's pit-
ted the worlds gainst oneother and there is no victor the words
the words are all so jumbled as a sex as sex can make you spit
and heave yet warm to the rest of the post- to the end of the road
and thumb yet warm to the risk of the road to the end of the post

~~

                                                                    . . .

. . . and now a pastoral with split rail fence beyond hay bale or three
of them limpid in the sun. she suns on rocks The New York Gorge
where the pools are reminiscent of their smells of are reminiscent of
Pennsylvania . . . . . . or for example in other words let me make this
make this tangible, somehow or as tangible how as tangible as i may
make it words do faile, reminiscent of a tonic failed by its succulence
into the stink of something between spiderweb and spiderscotton or
or the damp chutes of a denimin basement's stuck in a passageway or
perhaps the yolkrot of asparageal August. the pools are warm and in

warmth betraying or intimating a kind of poison-process. we invite
ourselves in for we're hot and in refreshment's need yet we don't heed
the algeal the alkaline the alliterative or assonant the pastoral, the poem
i say, the pastoral or the poem i say in which a stupefied man roams on

~~

it's hard to concentrate on plain or pasture marooned in urbania i'm
of the pine of the shitbrook stink of upwards atrail in April, mostly
May when the trees are coming out when the last leaves are going in
when i muscle the outcroppings and the paving stones and the slope
driven upwards by what compels the paniculata in some other locale
some other territory my eyes see the girl sitting staring at what i have
to offer she couldn't make it out here she wouldn't last a second she
is too weak too pretty too joyous like the soft summit wind in frisée
on one of the more gentle lower peaks my eyes are the scree's colour,
don't sit looking at me so, i have so little to give shitbrook stink May
or April when the pleasant autumnal's long since met its death throe
and the dust of male plants dust of male trees in the air's assaulting
the ill-prepared the brown tilt of scree look not at me look elsewards
stay away here stay lower stay joyous stay still and still tiny breeze stay

~~

still as marginalia i rise to a morning unfettered by metre unbound
from governance the cascade in the notch, the meander of a vine,
the glance or grace of sunshine on rock as whatever force sees fit

and even more importantly her hair that's always devastating a mine
fire in which many would be killed but for her stealthy rescue at dawn
and at dawn i am roused by not too often birds not every poem's got
to have trees yet so many do and so, does she love me or my window
does it need cleaning the dust of errata's gotten to it's stricken its face
struck do you realize one can begin a journey with rules of the road
and then come to the desert river and lose the impetus to circumvent
the escape of their very own life and then merely turn around turn to
the darker horizon and walk back. and there is no shame in such is
there?, or is the one waiting in the sunset's opposite direction gonna
fight when you write of cascades in which you show up at a later date

~~

as if in a glow i give off to all my friends a mightie love or else or they
would seek a new grove in which to study the ant, mighty ant, pitiable
ant and woeful ant of the post-never period in which art is the bygone
and all we've got left is a forest of clotheslines and where's the organic
in such a forest as this my my we've woven trouble's threadbarren era
the monument scene to the left and through trees deep the vista of city
of friendly drunkenness and fruit of holding hands with some stranger
an art student some twenty-two or twenty-three and always in her work
nude or cupping an ermine against her breasts always the wonderfully
and slowly decaying realness of a forest of my youth. and where are you,
friends, to make me want to keep wandering, it's your job after all. you'd
better be there when i need you're the paperweight atop these trillions these
uncountable billions of fuckedly scattering and skirmishing pages of mine

~~

and out over the gorge, slow-billowing and sifting cold from warm air
in simmering and in wafting the papers skeet along the edges of cliff
and high over the rushing waters of a place so frequented so photo'd
as to be qwerty. the avid walker is never surprised by such terrain yet's
always fascinated to see for the hundredth time or so the absolute ruin.
when he was younger he built forts in the woods and lit their thatches
with solvent and matches procured from a grandfather's tinderbox
cellar, wookworking enclave ensconsed in an outbuilding, or somesuch
place in similarity and fraternity with the dualist concepts of creation/
destruction. he now fondles driftwood on a shore thankfully unbrained
for it knows not the suffering and annihilation it's soon to endure come
hurricane season. this very beach belches up trinkets and treasures and
the walker loves such things these simplicities and is bored by them and
is truly at the ocean to witness the storm kill the beach and himself.

~~

kick the stone over a rocking horse can be built in three days given time
and proper materials and tools, a stepstool's the Delaware of projects
and a pebble the Alaskan wilderness when viewed from a vantage certain
the stone kicked into a chasm is one of the many beetles living in colony
in the collapse of a horse's brain near the mennonite barn near a gulch
near a town with "Gulch" in its name utterly removed from our excursion
into afternoon sex i mean i wish to tell all the men about your skin and
not the way it feels or its colour or smell or taste but its trajectory. stone

kicked into a ravine exerts positive downward force upon the air even
the ground, eventually if slightly and that is your skin at three afternoon
as you lay beneath me and when men talk they ask a friend *did you fuck
her* they mean *did you destroy her*. stone kicked into a ravine took a while
to reach its unfortunate position on the path to meet the boot and horse
assembled and shellacked on a calm August day in a cobwebby workroom

~~

i want the most certain point which is, the end of whatever road final post
to a friend torn and taped at the aorta's blood loss summer for the woman
who's got to love something so she turns to a caterpillar for governance
and how, how is Hart staring into his wife's eyes this moment? hey collect
grass wastings, thine little empty flower cups. they are as orange as azure.
they are as big as my hand is lexical. this world is going to be a mechanism
rigged with boatwire, sprigrew, floatrow and hemmingtrim. because there
there my friend the words say so because here they come and eddy water-
like because water exists but does not for it's not formalist. the girl i dream
is dreaming about being on a trail with me, is she in her eyes or withal?
at the footbridge between scream and whisper is a moss-malignant sign
-post scurvied by graffiti and having been forever ignored and man, that's
a thing of beauty to traverse to rupture to finding the final beyond the end
and this is the so-and-so of exchange i suppose in met eyes of the lovers

~~

some men lecture on beauty others try very hard to define to identify
and then to obliterate it in all its places and all its guises. emptylea,
floral Pennsylvania byway in the Alleghenies, past parked pickups
and gun buddies, we drove to the toppled railroad bridge and i like
that it fell that the valley floor was sent a warning. some men beauty
won't want won't find or seeke others are allergic to the maritime or
the genital, the celestial or the faunal, these being common hiding spots
where pleasure is to be found—in the jib in the arch in the writhe in
the way a star steeps in our black as night wears on in the tongue of
a pet showing its love the only way she knows how. indeed it does
it appears beauty has been equated here to pleasure and so shall it be,
do you have any better ideas? byway comes to thence to stall and over-
ridden motor, breakdown in the midst of midst and thence the well let's
talk of firewood's smell of what this all means of break out the wine

~~

once was afraid my lower-case i you make me important like a calendar.
carry me like a reed-basket of water over the pinions of landscapes
blasted by heat and then i will know where i belong. in a stream-of-
ideas i would hasten to add i hate money and would rather receive mulch
and that i like dry humour, hate the slapstick of the commonplace. please
come into the woods with me o eremitica the impulse to have been for-
gotten. o sayeth i this prayer in archaica for dignified words are all i can
use to get the seriousness across the riverway laconic we lay and near it
and whisper this poem and then mean it and deep in the back of all this
i don't want you here at all. you have somewhere better to be, i know it.

smokestacks and breakers, who knows what you should prefer, anything
but this. i wish your rigidity to cease with convention—leave me become
free form like a dryad spilling all over the trunk of an oak oh dear pretty
one make something good happen somewhere else i know you can do it

~~

standards and ballads else pastorals seeke within and for solace to find
no further they now this woman and forest and gorge but as concepts of mind

SONGEUR

You look egg shell in brown the stand there on a tree-lined street
as you glance toward a distant park We must stop walking together
soon for the rain will come back Did you pressurize your special tree
trunk as I witnessed last autumn When I had no idea who you were
When I was ripe for dismissal like an anvil a top hat a horse's shoes
a monad Why did you enter my life Zebra herded out of its travel
for children's eyes to witnesseth Easter Morning come spilling previous
night into memry and for all a new salvation a brand of Sunday kitchen
cast light upon knives with baby's breath handles Why did you Sidewalk
dusted with the all-time most vicious and abundant pollen the malfunction
of signage the closed street's lane a solitude is an abstraction not in Paris
where slow stroll is de rigeur and you weren't with me But you talk Paris
all the time and what do you think I will be able to do Why do I give in
What does this sketch this scribbling on the cafe napkin symbolise What
is a sign or fate or everything for its reason but stones as empty of mass
of content as a library is as empty of solutions For whom do you watch at dusk
when the willows frame the stars so theaterifically when mist is life's meaning
I know you watch You are the kind to do so just look at your eyes' pensee
and nonscatter They fix on some irresolute past in which all you'd eat alone
each evening was oats some indeterminate future You'd look good with a smoke
but you don't do so and to your credit Why do you cause me to dream up scenes
like these Or like the one in which we trade lines along a bay and the sky is dregs
like always and the ducks are May's October's ours Swimming hole up north

nestled aside in a brook on Kinsman Ridge up high It took me several attempts
to make it up there Once I was turned back by the top of thunder as grievous
and grief-stricken as a rabbit hutch overgrown with the loss of a past in which
men bred rabbits for show and for meat for pleasure and for grandsons to learn
about care and tending And now look at my lump of failure in the guise of paper
upon which words sprayed contemplate the slow death of morality's tiny and of
a pain and a depth we've all got and it's what makes sculpture so and it's what
and it's what makes paintings so And these scenes in which we act out a thing
so untenable and far-removed from any universe we will ever know these eat
til they are full Do you know the parable of the worm the brick and the ointment
Neither do I but the three actors sound terrible together like rigid tempera's grip
on untreated cardboard the egg gone sour and the pigment mixed piss-poorly
Are you here to help my maudlin drip out a bit faster than usual Look a stone
it skips the surface of the pond For whom do you watch at dusk from beneath
the black iron awning of a building abandoned storefront emptied glass intact
but business vacated For whom How you can stand for thousands of hours
in silence and only with me is a home in the swallow's unrecognized willow
The bird returning to a place it's never known but for what its instinct and its
jam-like neurons tell it You have been here and here you will stay and here
you will have to make some kind of subsistence view of the meadows the larks
don't have it so good The grapple and debate Wasn't I somewhere better or
don't I belong to some other place And then the wind kicks in and the bird
the bird forgets the trifles and needs to settle in Needs to Do you green
like a word cut from esoteric notepad rooftop What processes have you
Look at your shoes they are ocean avenue brown In the brook a churn a sand
brought down from the high peak and still going to the bottom of the sea
Is that how the narrative goes Indeed and you keep coming and walking in scenes

toward me and I am sad for I can't picture the sea at all The thought of the chute
of brook my favorite mountain range's sonorous but I can't picture the sea.

WRITTEN IN A RAINSCAPE

It's my rotten endearment.
It's my rotten endearment to places.
It's my rotten endearment to places I'm not.
It's my rotten endearment to places I'm not, places.
It's my rotten endearment to places I'm not, places far off.
It's my rotten endearment to places I'm not, places far off but places.
It's my rotten endearment to places I'm not, places far off but places I need.
It's my rotten endearment to places I'm not, places far off but places I need just as
It's my rotten endearment to places I'm not, places far off but places I need just as my rotten
It's my rotten endearment to places I'm not, places far off but places I need just as my rotten endearment
It's my rotten endearment to places I'm not, places far off but places I need just as my rotten endearment to people
It's my rotten endearment to places I'm not, places far off but places I need just as my rotten endearment to people I can't have
It's my rotten endearment to places I'm not, places far off but places I need just as my rotten endearment to people I can't have or treat
It's my rotten endearment to places I'm not, places far off but places I need just as my rotten endearment to people I can't have or treat with
    my harsh light.

~~

What's your problem, fucker?
It's my rotten endearment. Mind your business, metal.
You sound like rain pushing a cup through a jive alley.
You sound like a busybody eloquence from window to window.
You sound like rain, you are rain, you were rain

just as I was once a stump inside my mother.
I grew to be an agnostic but not an angry one. Red
suits me poorly, burgundy is my colour. I like you in a blue cap.
Wear it. Always carry a baguette of steel in your pupil. City,

oh grave city, who are me to tell you how to be? What's
the temperature?
Where's my gunpowder
I say, I talk the rain smells
like onions here. I had places
to go and either went or didn't.
I have no places to go, I am marooned.
I can choose to like it I can choose to find someone to fuck here.
I can get angry at my skin, at my miasma, at every type of thought
and I likely will for I'm as sick of this stasis as the sky of the sun
and the sun of "sunset," which is a word that enrages sense away
for the sun sets not it subdues itself from vantage A and into vantage B!,
this is my lofty science.
This is my lofty love to chat with brick and rain's ground metal
pocking my particular sky.
I never saw a flower,
I refuse to see them.
I refuse to paint flowers
I refuse to pearl my petal or skin your orange,
learn how to do it yourself.
I bathe sometimes on Sunday.
This Sunday's a heavy cardstock—

I judge the day by its clouds

not by the happy faces beneath them

or within them! *What's your problem, fucker?,*

don't you believe in heaven? A previous incarnation of me

did. A future one will. In this street I stroll around looking on the walls for

tiny scratchings to see who's been there. I like nicknames

I like perusing the skyline for suicide divers, I want to tell them to stay put

and read the applause of the crowd gathered at the buildings' bases.

It means you have been rewarded by not jumping

with an extra ten to fifty years to wonder whether you should've jumped

when you had the chance. Get your mind off yourself. Driftwood

and rope, pungency and radio waves. So much in our world,

manufactured matchstick tip, ready to go wrong at any moment.

This is why I am standing in the rain, it makes me suspicious

and I like to feel this way. It makes me suspicious of happy people

they must be frauds don't they want to be somewhere else, someone else,

be with someone else? Don't they want a cigarette? A bottle of Pernod?

A book of nudity written by the young hotshot who enjoys poems?

A leaf of baytree grown with ninety-eight-point-eight-percent documented care

by a sixty-two-year-old widower in 33° 7′ N 117° 5′ W?

Anything besides?

Now to turn inward because I'm bored by thought.

I want to walk to the water with my special someone.

She is a boat.

She might become what is known as flippant.

She conducts erasure on my vulgar thoughts to arrive at a safety point.

We will stand on a jetty in a rain similar to today's

and I will confide in her how bad a person I am
and she will tell me *no, you're wrong* and I'll scoff
and she'll touch me and I'll use that as my in
and slip my tongue in her mouth and later
I will slink her out of her skirt and see what I want to see.
I will, rain. I will. What will you do tonight
but haunt the seaboard?

SONG OF LOSS AND HOPE

I won't put on the stoic face and grit, I won't
sleep again I won't care about the wind I won't and the oranges
of the front lawn's palm basket. I will think of every new friend as a weed,
I will wander
like I care about the sproutlings tossed from lime trees.
I hear decline's guitar
to which I am receptive.
The world is a spring of fuck.
I bloody you because I hate you with all my fingernails can muster when clawing the veneer
off a hotel armoire. I needed to check in
when I realized I couldn't sleep in my own house
because the tendency to burn it down wouldn't subside.
I rip your papers students I stick the pages with spit
I think you less useful than masking tape in rain.
I want the mountains of New Hampshire to wield themselves against the Midwest and crush the heft of boredom out here on the Buffalo plain.
I want the mountains of New Hampshire to wield themselves against the South and crush the cars and sludge the pools of bible-thumping
    perverts in frocks.
The mountains of New Hampshire will resurrect themselves and they will endure to remind me
of whatever of which I want to be reminded. It's up to me.
And if I want to be tempted, I will be
and if I want to give in thusly I shall.
You can stand by and watch.
You can draw the curtain when five comes and the lamps begin flickering on and I'm not there,

I'm off on a summit plastered on white wine stored in a used water bottle
jammed into my overstuffed backpack. I'll puke on the granite slabs and scoop and toss it
out into dawn, toss it onto all the world of corporeal shit. This one's for the stupid president,
this one's for the unintelligent and visionless leaders of business,
speaking in cliché and euphemism,
this one's for the newspaper copy editor who doesn't catch the semi-colon,
this one's for the cheating athletes,
this one's for the religious perverts doing ill to the name of Thomas Merton,
this one's for the women who scrubbed my heart of feeling until I became the supremest asshole
in the Northeast, but one at least with charmingly deep brown eyes.
This one's for myself because I'm disgusting. Not worth this vomit,
not fit for this summit, one that Thoreau was once straddling.
They named a waterfall after Henry David Thoreau and it's down there
in the valley in the shadow of this mountain, as it were.
This one is for people who don't read Thoreau. Here, take it, fucker!,
what else will you have to call an idea in this world?
I'll probably keep drinking and you'll wonder why I didn't come home
and then you'll remember I like to go out and mourn the loss
of all the loves I was perilously close to falling into,
of all the first places I second-placed into,
of all the loves I fell into that had to end for whatever eye-scouring reason,
like the last one. She stared so goddamned passionately
and I returned the favour And it was all out of something foreign,
like love but even better—devoid of the lust. I never thought of her
as something to attain. If anything, she attained me. I felt subservient and inferior
in her presence.
I liked that

and I liked the eye contact.
Goodbye.
I want the entire Presidential Range, which is dozens and dozens of miles in length
and many miles wide, and many trillions of tonnes, laden with tree and scree
and erratic and brushpatch,
to back itself up onto me
and put me in the dark.
Heretofore unknown
dark.
It has the magic to do so.
I've not the power to command it.

~~

Let me show you where the rocks fell from the mountain,
and you can tell me they'll grow back again.
Tell me you'll get in the car and go north with me, good
riddance to all the clusterfuck bullshit.
We'll hold each other at the scenic vista and the wind
will drown out the idling engine.
As long as you have the ability to speak
and the desire to speak to me
I will love you. The mountains would, too,
love you, that is, and they will
when I shepherd you there.
Pack only one bag,

it's all taken care of.
You look at me knowingly, because
I'll pick cherries with you
and sit quietly with you.
Needless motion and action
are out of our question
and that you appreciate.
You hold my hand and it's the moon—
it's the birdfeeder assaulted at dawn
by the entire flock of sparrows
in the whole state coming
at once. Parting your lips just
slightly when you kissed me,
I sensed that was by design. You,
you're more knowing than you think.
You plied me—this is why you'll return.
I'll make sure to have a large basket
of pineapple and grapes prepared for you.
I'll make sure to have cut away the death
that shrouds my mind and my work,
my eyes and my outlook————broadest sky
over the peaks at which we stare
from the scenic overlook, the car idling
like a coughing October child
mittens clustered with snow—
please raise the rocks again
reverse the landslide

tell me you can do it,
come back to me
and tell me you can do it.

CHAPTER

Tarpaulin I call my home this stormy world.
Windswept tarn on the high ridge my ocean
always gray no landfall in sight earth's dropped
off. How do we rebuild—before rains arrive,
after starry romance is clouded over. Stray
hair, eight aeons ago you held onto me. My
shoulder. I saved you in a secret box, if only
to remember I need forget you at all costs.

PISCES

salvage lot lakeshore
of post-tryst i try
to see your daisy

i resist employed
vigour toward poems
in this new time

women clear fences
of vine move slowly
like sinking stilts

invited to scotch parties
i prefer to smoke
and pick mallow

no magical river ever
to find forehead
mine, or flower same

staring down water
there's not enough
clouds round earth

TARN STAR LAKE

Star Lake is no
lake
it is a tarn
called Star Lake.
It is shaped
like a star
thus it is
Star Lake
(the tarn).
It straddles
a high ridge
it looks on
all of us;
when sun
glistens rock
along its fringe
or in its shallows
the light bounces
back up up up
to the cloud
and a reflection
of you and all
you do, and us

and all we do,
duly radiates on
the cloud's belly
and is transmitted
for all to see.
This is why
a tarn named
Star Lake means
so much to me
and why it's
the subject here
because it matters.
It matters to deer
lost on the foggy
top. It matters
to hawks for
bearing. It matters
to god because it
made it. It matters
to earth because
the tarn remains
and earth is good
at ruining useless
things. Thus, the
tarn is useful (I
have proven that
or illustrated that

point, at least). You
like ice? Come up
to the tarn it will
feed you endless
it will I swear. I
see that I swear
upon the name
of god the first
time in my life,
this is how serious
the ice's there.

NINEAINS

moss affects travel by foot i am not into the city not now
at least. i know i went around the big dam in upper reach
but presbyterians made me do it i know satellites' amouria
i know seed smell at night when the neighbours pass out
coffee tins, when they expect showmanship and gravity
and who else blank verse tired white ship of poetry but ye
to come to rescue at sea off on my tiny morsel of island
clung to language's pretty bog eyes of irresolute downturn
of all there's left here's an X and a Y and fuck the map

~~

pretty firework my only ever did you hear humidity crawl
or was it the bug of the verb that itchd the grain called eye
the pupil exacting and polygamous thus you scrawld in ink
on the meadow of i miss you the missive *now you're dead*
and *i couldn't wait until you passed because my guilt subside it*
will and *your lock of hair dyed darkish brown shall i singe*
like seventeen of every one-thousand-thirty catalpas near mood
near firehood and then *now will i rest yes in the arms as it were*
of my lover he is great with a pitchfork he loves all our senators

~~

here is the ghazal my allergy here is my wheat field burned
youthfulle and vigrous the harte crosseth the field spurned
you know i'm fucking my wife right now reader and write
writes my other hand do it efficiently like sunrise which's
meagre when thought of as texture for man has perfectd
god and all he could ever hope to create ask the president
he will telle you ask my wife scratching me now in pleasure
oh does that make you uncomfortably jealous—fuck you
you had a chance this ghazal me and you's wrapd up ethan

~~

script in which scenes end as curtain's raised what the fuck
the point's what is the goddamned point of a lover of sky
dappld grackle calls resonant there what reason but torture
and punishment offer me some reason besides oh you can't
but the sea is swill on afternoons like this you are some there
i am some here temprate as spit as dire as heaving ah burden
thine whites sharp as summits in december i love being tied
and bound until blood vessels issue surrender stove ignition
clicking someone downstairs is failing i'm up here dreaming

~~

i'm a lover of vicia sativa do you know that's exotic waste
garden weeds i've got empathy serrulata linaria communis
dusk falls upon you i see from a belfry's rail i pray i was

rolled neath our quilt of planets full on from this vantage
her pretty red shirt's charm necklace fondled what is left
by an overturned wheelbarrow fuck williams this is mine
what's left at the lot corner's my recent passéd harbour
dredged and dumpéd she's a mayfly of all pretty yellows
she flies around this dusky backyard i sit smoking no end

~~

may's end i know what it is to be used dry air moved
out and humid's in fashion get your tepid voice off
the floor i know you regret me just say it cross me out
of the daybook hotel balcony vision calendar from your
goosebumps daydreams i know i am boring you know
i am bad for you this was the worst persimmon torrid
red but bruiséd from get-go eaten with cinnamon
book of brown earth what we were is the old kind of mud
clustered from boots sunk once in a trail leading nowhere

~~

the city looked regal this morning's buildings clusterd
and tall huddld like friends in humid vapours a lake
well beyond and beneath these we walk atop springs
secret if only to fall through if only the goldenrod's
got to go it's a weed i feel angry about its being here
changes physical syntactical and paradigmatic in place

my new kitchen coffee experience sun afew blinds
no calm no i'd lay for hours no you'd tend to me
you were sent to this city to punish and to tantalize

~~

are you happy i guess sure i must have been skedaddled
goodbye are you on earth anymore if a tree falls goodbye
pushed about at torso by a rough lake swell can't steady
goodbye awkward's moonlight between decrepit garages
goodbye deserted's a forest trail the deer've all been shot good
bye to all of them and to leaves i photographed as you stood
marvelling at my sappiness be honest you never wanted me
bored woman did you ever really you never confess silently
so quietly hands in your lap you sit hiding rifle and ax

~~

connection's gone dead's cabin ridgetop turn on the lone sun
let it in No on the other hand keep it all out the river's swelld
and needs all the goodwill we can give all my words are runny
in disposition winter is coming connecticut maine to vermont
massachusetts rhode island new hampshire it's making its way
and i don't know where to put this yet dearest figurine and pretty
my shelf for you else the hammer to you all the rivers swelld out
there stay on your side and i've got mine i can see your oblivion
you dance and smile i kick stones blow piss on fallow territory

SILENT MORNING

she asks what I carry,
it's thistle

ask not what I carry

in each dewdrop
a cracked branch

have I wronged you?

I can't say that I care
for her face's gone a

shower of dust, a light

-starved exit sign, shards
of abandoned orphanage

NON-LINEAR PASTORAL DEPRESSIVE

no way do we stand in gloucester
no the path isn't as winding as
i'd like it to be that way, you
could stay with me a bit longer
sip my milk a bit slower linger
like goldenrod clinging to summer
in the death of october when it's all
down, when the cows are otherside
and the barn door's doored tight
no ocean breeze's here just mingle
of dogwood and tinge of august
as sky connects us to an else other-
wise and upward, up there and it's
the thing i've got in my chest
when you stop by the pike near
the peavy by the brook, and wipe
your chin with your wrist water's
drip i see your blanket of birch
where you'd have had me but
identity called and you went back
to the labours at hand, i know this
i saw you scurry back up the hill
cringing as if to be chastised for
walking the lane, away, off toward

against the hill behind us not in gloucester, no some hill in hill country we're in,
its milk-gray habitus, outbuildings trundled by sky that is to say by a terminus
whereat we shall evaporate, it's milk-gray and terrible out here save your stare
but you don't know you are no dowager, you are no simplesse, you are a difficulty
akin to linen and line, posthole and the clouds like stapled incessantly to universe
and daily, we're on some hill and feeling surprise for the first time today, minuet
o minuet o thin thing, gentil and douaire of candied light spindled, evergreens off
and milés off the barrenness of homestead, whey, muted sky, heft to the nose of cow,
your breasts not yet even not yet suggestive. say, this is a massif we've got now miss
my my. you adopt the riles of beauty well and what to say but that i stare resultant,
i recall a coast-side castle i never will see and inside, a botanical museum and there
some vernation and in your tresses, how they float, i mean, the ferns' croziers. ah
the breeze that would sheath us would you caress me and here, this is how. hand,
taken in hand, middling duty cast off and if only so that our eyes'd write lines all
afternoon and all over our skin like goldenrod clinging to summer in the death of
october and did you know about my mountains?, how they are holy in some way
like the manner of strawberry is holy or how that fruit does music to colour. you
should come with me. this is the story: there is a roundabout in downtown and if
the night's got its green tinge then you'll know god is throwing a fit he can't stop
your arrival to me and in the thicket i'll be having washed my hands of the gesso
and the charcoal, having prepared several canvases for tomorrow for the afterward
where you'll sit drinking a tea miles away and i'll douse myself in hand-wringing,
chain-smoking. i'll railing the widows watch lean way up there for you and wait
and then we can finally watch the boats slide by, yet again, and the tidal basin's

the royals and the deeps in each blue
flutter of rivulets within which i was
not born, music was strewn, water
our bread without knife our pestle
without mortar our verb inactive
in one of the trillion's array of pages
like proclamations of love's sentence

constellations of whitecaps will remind us of dandelion and limestone scree, these
of the hill upon which we first met. the shore and the pool and the boats sliding by
must be in gloucester where from your expression i see you too would like to stand.
i have nothing that tangible to offer no and there is no way. see that barn atop there
i gotta go there and i don't know, it's heavy and it's hard. it's bright and it'll rain,
you're listening right now and tomorrow you're gonna be a breeze in the rainstorm's
bitching against my shutters and i'll try to open them and they're just gonna resist.

O HOLY HILL

so sullen curse of persimmon so red
the bushel basket ere full and spillt
can you humble a clumsy man flimsy
from his deepest inside, trip him up
cherry tree expanse the rows to traverse
with orchards hues of dusk are deeper
quiver, quiver abandon'd felled in the oak leaves
the deer got away into blueberry patch rancoria
the wind is thruway violent tonight leaves know
doubtless they don't sail or coast they clutter
otherwise slate-rain parcel of city's night
you run downhill toward me switchbacks
don't matter you run and run and then
restless sleep while our little vessel seas us
and waves can be considered hills as such
and kiss me we'll be horizonéd soon Love

IN THE SUMMER OF WEDDINGS AND OF DEATHS

surprise!   the river's stopped rolling,
the city lonesome has stopped twinkling,
there are no stars reflected,
there is no love for the unattainable girl,
there is no sickness killing off my family,
the childless haveth in tatters their spirits,
i can run around yelling out her name

The willows drinketh the freshet and swiftly
The city a mockery of horizon and constellation
The stars The stars The stars The stars
The love for the unattainable girl Ah her dress
The sickness killing my grandfather O yes
The childless consoled by their reflections
I can't even walk, my friend, I rot I rot I rot

INTELLECTUAL STANZAE

what means it hue that
she hates me cloud
is hue of window
through which far off
a man cooking
for a woman
down in London
for the weekend
is cooking through
a side of meat

what means its dried
territory discourteous

the many afraid of
multisyllabics | like rocks
about a landscape can
seem | in an ecotextual
system or sense | killing

motorous sky
what means it | to
particulate a sky to

fragment as a coaxial
sky's median message
what means its rain
but harm what else
but canyons resist
colourfast territories
sound in parlance
in timbres stiff
work back as if
with wrists the
hardest rainsiest
disarboureate days
when glass | glass's
what's a creek to be
but if nothing steady

language is notorious
a side of meat
motorous sky
but if nothing steady
language is notious
and notional a window
luminal | glass's rattle
it's, sort of. cooking
meat and writing poems
in timbres stiff
or laxid aflorality

the union of dictionaries
by which the parcels
are rigged and plenitudinous
and juried

with which we ply a reality
of lovers and karst, she
mayst love me cloud
beaches, states with
an official flower each
each with cities with
official hats

LIFE IMITATES CENTO

a dreamer of pictures | i run in the night
has never made much sense, ?, i love

this singer's politics, invention,
integrity but this line is a rabbit's

having been flayed as the one at six
i saw in grandfather's animal pen

its head had been guitared into oak
a block hewn from the lot

.....

i could be happy the rest of my life
with a cinnamon girl like the girl

with whom i have chai and into
whose autumndry eyes i decide

i need be executed

.....

ten silver saxes | a bass with a bow
thigmotaxis thanatopsis Bryant's boring

ars shitetica this new poetry give new
year's fluttery, confetti's a couplet at
which stare through her whispers' space

.....

you see us together chasing the moonlight
you should mind your own business

    Afide:

    my love, your autumndry eyes
    my plague,

    i am affixéd to a brown room.

    to the impudent window-rattle, and to
    the guitar which's sic'd on me, i am affixéd.

    exeunt exeunt
    my love from
    whom i am sick

PAROLIER

[The cloud is . . .]

The cloud is a poetic theory.
Grass is several miles away.
Both are beyond horizons,
horizons we shall never touch
with our breath. With our shells,
minions of a favourite beach.
The dying bell of dry ocean,
the tiring smell of empty canvas,
the attack of my belovéd's stare—
that's a cloud in itself, which
cuts the arrays of sunbeams . . .

[Le nuage est une théorie poétique.]

[She . . .]

She is frustrated from reaching
what I am, a long roadway.
We wander and often, trees
interrupt. She is, my friend,
so arid. The skies dry. She walks
next week for bread. My friend,
she will eat bread for a month.
My friend, rain is an invitation
for you to leave the cloisters
within which you tally strings,
red and white. Her face, friend,
you must see, but it troubles me
through the myriad bramble.
She is frustrated and will one day,
perhaps, rest in my arms, road
having been traversed, limbs
and branches having been parted.

[Elle est frustrée d'atteindre
ce que suis je, une longue chaussée.]

[Lovely . . .]

The word's used by some   *[Le mot est employé par nous]*
and as an inside joke.
The word means an apple
or otherwise, chocolate
or otherwise, something
else I care not to explain
but rather, something
I would rather taste,
her mouth, for instance.
Her mouth, explicitly.
I want hers on mine
as it was down in Paris,
in the Oregon gulch.
I mustn't lose what it is
that makes this word
what it is, to both of us.

[Apologia . . .]

Accept my apology: the window is large   *[Acceptez mes excuses: la fenêtre est grande]*
and: throughout, the biggest town at night
and: within, everything they say. For you.
Accept my apology: I shall remember
to close the curtains. I imagine you doing so—
I stand in a field and look up, Look!, _____
is closing the curtain on me and, look now,
my face and my future are sour like snow.

ENDEARMENT

I.

One poem begins in Maine
and ends in another state,
another begins life as a guide
and ends a scourge, a plague.
One poem begins in French
and is rendered in English,
another is a second, a mite,
a sandlet, almost as desolate
as a hidden mountain trail.
One poet begins with love
and trails off, losing it
in the sun, finding it again
in a cold autumn, toward
the end of his book. Begins
he with the picture in mind:
the girl for whom he longs
who smiles and only for him,
from the end of a beach
on one bank of a strait
irrelevant to crowds.

She is alone with him
on this beach, smiling
and together they
throw shells to
their destinies
of perpetual travel
of eternal hardship.
The picture is awash,
like a sketch, but through
the meander of mind and distraction,
he makes out her lovely eyes
as so many young male artists have.
He fancies himself unoriginal,
thereby deciding to write difficultly
so as to enliven the old sentiment.
So as to draw a crowd in yellow,
whether galoshes or water-coats
for when the coast gets on them.
He writes and makes the chase
for the image, trying to impress her
speaking to her through words
making her present through words
but she is off somewhere with better to do
than to sit with a pen, penning him odes.
He wonders whether she thinks of him
and wonders how to incorporate same
and again, is unwowed by his nature

much too human, too pedestrian.
The poem begins on a beach
and features two lovers and degrades
into a pastiche of ironic styles
borne of the 1950s. She becomes, well,
less relevant in the poem than in his vision,
his daydream. He then disservices her,
his beloved. When will he learn?
When will the little boys, the little
poets, ever learn about things attainable
or not attainable, learn about yearning
and that to engage in it causes pain
and many bad and disingenuous poems.
When will autumn come, and how'll
this one begin and how'll it end.
There is either she will embrace him
or she will not, and either way
autumn will march in gray
as ever like the staticky neige
of a crystal ball . . .

II.

Having watched cloud mutual
here to there passage's timely
sculpture park rust parametres

distance's verst its heft Tsvetaeva
hard travel I flail you cuckoo
this endgame supreme compleat
diaristic cookbook's futureal
mercuries. Hot, running cold,
awning collapséd British slang
in the everbush. How'd partnered
ivies smoke and thrush, trestle
bed of pinions and rails brookside
conjugal's confused it all for whom
do I lay and with whom, how love
sedges away from meaning's dread
convention, handbook lyrical made
for circus, for theatre, for river,
for all we give our cents a couple
flipside tails, toss and save heads
and molds and caboodle, and orbitals
rabbit endentured in nature skywise
an answer she bolded and awestook
misstruck with underline, crayon
handshake last dominion's apron
with the tail of yarn, self-control
and otherwise blippers and throttles
gainéd paradise with a flick, a bric
of cracked snowstorm tree and why
oh why october come you with down
of metal of mite in mode of destrode

and stepped-aside summer, which was
and ago so soft and modal in yellows
and ogle at particulate city's bridges
historic in vapidity's hallmarkish
americana the fool the eye a word
a la paintbrush handles' oiseaux
oliverian brook the brown signage
hand-carved craftsmade whine on
child you'll get not what ye want
you'll get what you need doubtful
love love is love is a cloud debarks
at three o clock what time will it
arrive in Buffalo from Paris when
drifting westward Atlantic claymation
automatic nope freshet static narrative
is all about the words is all about words
the love of words the scent of words
the build of words the prime of words
the might of words the dearth of words
the use of words the scope of words
the scrape of words the light of words
the ripe of words the dud of words
the cone of words the mule of words
the rid of words the give of words
the stride of words the scant of words
the fucked-up words endearing words
like her and me and poem and love.

III.

She's apart from him
and never comes,
like ur-winter.
She instills fear.
Come on, writer,
admit it. Use a verb
and show it. She
will never kiss you
again you know it.
The time? Fallow.
I think, or four p.m.
One can tell by the flood
which is always off by inches
or by the leafy acreage off east
drugging the horizon in brown.
I touched her once in a field
that will never wonder about it.
I saw her debate herself, losing.
These ideas we have about loss,
they are marginally cloud-like.
Loss is expressed by distance and
ideas, by proximities of little marks
on a page. There is the weight of meadow
in-between. Or the weight of seashore,
riverbank, mountain-top, wherever else

the lovers may have eaten foods.
The weight is the noun, and the verb,
well, the verb is loathe, as in the parting,
the need to have done so, the need to return
to a stale bed and a stale lover,
and the need to need.

PATRON SAINT GUNPOWDER

KINOGLAZ

No matter the latitude, dearest sky,
something ill-mannered's about you—

It might hold a staff and pace atop you
It might be rain, supreme toy and gray

It might like a tough wife be gravity's
balling you up It might be. Just might

But down here, the bottom, I'll get to it,
I'll get to the bottom of you and report

back. I had no dinner tonight an attempt
at clear thought monosyllabic in ease.

I can see through you whom I know
and have never met via balloon force

but I'm coming and I'm ruminating.
Cacti in a desert aahing matins upward

Birds zesting aloft from eaves and trees
We're all coming to find you god all of us

all of it. Storm the gate with matchsticks
we will. It will be violent when we find you.

AFTER TRUTH [GÖTTES]

Man is a turd of a god. This
thesis shall be advanced and
it has. His rivers are ridden
all to ends. He boats any way
and he can. It is a drat blasted
waste in the face of nothing
benign at all but all black all
out there and up there and
opaque and black and hidden.
Most evil man on earth inside
each other man trust burnéd
currency. You are an astute
reader you are of good spirit
you know the trope of chain
and bondage in savage lands
of torture by sea water omni-
cut and ever-present spill of
spit and semen's got it good
we really did. His scythe to
arm him and take him on out
to a sui generis homestead's
quiet from ever- and ur-danger,
man is shit at getting at god.

A few miles beyond's a swamp
thicket, at which we can lunch
on dead animal and dry colours
of the civilised art school sterility
of order and white dignity's gown
jump on in the trek is on the gnat
the leech both affixéd and forever.

ARS NIHIL

I think we write poetry to see what a dun flower might smell like,
what a razor meticulous in its upkeep spurs in the barnyard festivus,
to see what frost feels like expanding scrotum of morning, hillocks all
smooth with cow and or goat, I think this is a wonderful life we've got
because we can ejaculate and erase. I think we write poetry up all night
paperweighted as we are to lilac awards, I think there is a man wandering
up a driveway in my poem to be wandering up a driveway in my poem to be
and I know where to start, with the man sawing wood and then leaving
to a hole at or of which he can't even perceive. He just exits his workshop
and begins walking to reach my driveway's base, then up the angle toward
me and my home white nicety yellow clapboard New England noon-timeish
famous and well-practised. I think we write poetry cuz it comes like yknow
Halloween. I think that guy is still walking I think I will SHOCK THE FUCK
OUT OF YOU WITH NEEDLESS CAPS. I think we write poetry all bummed
because an iceberg is on the way and there's an orgy on the communication bridge
and we weren't invited. The dun flower I think it stinks I think it just might stink.

THREADS

1.

Lobster traps empty near Boar's Head
New Hampshire, orange baskets of false corn dread of a field in Rutland in Vermont
The other detritii of landscapes he helped trawl and ruin now hang in his den
Symbols without suffering and context, communication without challenge or flange
Clouds of memories burning hot junk, politicking and science co-mingling
The loss of a beloved once held close in a pasture, the clouds framed her head well
and made her as stark as any patron saint of gunpowder or five-part-harmony stageplay.

2.

Men with red ear lobes criss-cross a beach looking for a missing girl
A gourd mists as slowly as a deep desert waterspring boilt in a snap
A machine [   ] it stamp [1-2-3] it stamp [1-2-3] it stamp [1-2-3] it stamp [1-2-3]
A boxcar traverses, in the fantasy of a seven-year-old boy who's never seen Colorado,
        a mountain range tattered with greens and browns his father, had he access
        to the son's dream, would recognize as the property of the alpine vales of
        Switzerland, near a pair of ski flying ramps, as those in Werner Herzog's
        poetic short documentary, *The Great Ecstasy of the Woodcarver Steiner*
which in its American guise is called "*The Strange Ecstasy of the Sculptor Steiner*"
and this is false because there's nothing strange about defying universal law
but to a public that demands ease of experience. In addition, Walter Steiner

was less a sculptor but indeed a woodworker. He remarks, at the film's start,
as we view him in his workshop latheing and coaxing a tree stump,
of the peculiar nature of found wood—his looked, to paraphrase,
exploded outward and this was with what he needed to *work*.
He had to *deal with* nature, as he had difficulty dealing with gravity,
the limitations of the frail human body, and the malevolence of God
who always chastises those who attempt beyond this dreck,
who always casts down lovers by causing their bodies to part
and by making even their mingled sweat dry into a cool air
of past, history, and half-lost ineffable motherland.
The hundreds of mille-neuf-cents of fashionable tin helixes.
The washed cottage-front green brick and beggars' mortar.
The ruffled ocean happily failing the pull of the moon.
The thirst of my penis I am not special some willowtree embankment hollow,
I am the taker of indigo and liferaft the donor of rift and light shaft—
see how I try to illuminate tin thimbles in elms at night
and usually falter oft distracted. Three wolves.
Your warbler on the roof. Life is a delightful oneiric film.
We almost hit another airplane. Orderless is everything;
there is no surrealism, just criss-crossing contrails in blue space
and, walking the desert to and fro, sometimes men with red faces.

f minor seven is the girl i love
f minor seven her darknesses
f minor seven her wine skin tastes
like f minor seven quiet by brookside
street ends i'm on the wall backt
cut to the sailboat
diegetic moans from the mournful symphony
across a valley a road in which a young girl's tresses
blow fire went out and the stillness of evening mills
frozen pastures strangers red sleeping stars' zenith
cut to the bath tub
of the little daughter's first love, water
her barrettes lay without debt on the tile
later in life by a man's side she'll spend her will
to make marriage work and god hope it will
cut to the aerialine an iron pot with wings
cut to the cliffs cut to the colour brown
cut to the husk of damned family
cut to the novel that is the son of depth
cut to the skyline of a forlorn desert
sequential series of a forlorn chord
which in the end is a rural sandpit or the like
fringed by gentian pine, sensitive friend to hurt
tossd for years by the bluster of an eastern winter
the music of all lives imperfect

SUBNARRATIVE OF NANTUCKET

You wanted to write about the bedspread
and its sentence-green itemic stitching but:
and here's the hinge: something in light-
Canadian arctic front long streeted's winter

Long-leggéd inspiration cut the low branch
so's you can make it to the swamp in time
to hear the grasshopper pulpit
Limes form irascibility They are high You are below

A poem latched between wood blocks's
squeezed into an accordionesqueature
The air's bassline is the bedspread,
coursing ideas the legs warmd beneath

INTERRUPTED NARRATIVE: NEIGE

Having never been not in love with a woman
but it's the piano of snow in Montréal
and so know to allow myself myself
when a nicety ship paradeth by say
her frilly have no idea how to play but pound my desk
when "It Makes No Difference" is on by The Band
featuring Garth Hudson on arp Richard Manuel's
there too The rains fall down on my door
It was the most important glance in my repertoire
used on half-hippy women within reach coffee
and cigarette ownership, highway in Sedona's
goodbye, lover
I am the enneagram number four and you,
rock-solid heft of ruined collage-burlap on my doorstep
deserted me humid gray August day smelling of chemical
repeal cubism dadamatissimo ta neige piano of snow three below

INTERRUPTED NARRATIVE: MARIENBAD

She wore a yellowstripe dress dressier than August.
She wore it the Saturday I met her, some dumb look.
Yes, Maricel, there is a stoved chicken for you.
Think of the order of the famous still Resnais, yes?,
conical shrubs and mathematical universe actors.
Cigarettes are not good for cows but get ingested.
Not good for Michigan or Montparnasse are coal mines.
Some of these are flooded. Look low, stare into the wreck
mirrors. Pilings, slag and burn, free association is winter's
bastard mountainside blowdown illegible & unlineaged trees
devastated by forty-below and katabatical damnation. Phew.
I tried to get into her blouse, texture of certain light breasts
I got the fascination, Whitman Tsvetaeva I picked my spots
don't read useless newsprint poesie, go to the well you fuck
you need to learn harmony from fledgling hardwater tresses
and subterranean micron nailhead hatchlings flitting to-fro
so as to make it home. Her dress was on her breasts, belly
I will see never she likes airport novellas her air of danger's
Los Angeles turbidity. Beryllium kite's in the trunk I drink
as sun, bitching dot, churns eighty-two-billion boredoms

DISJUNCTIVE FIELD [ARTILLERY]

I have brought you a slag heap in a ribboned lingerie box from Paris
pow, bam, bang, kerplunk my god, from where do I get this anger, kid?,
maybe we are products, like diluted meats who knows arresting skies
of the northeast dead american cities full of nobodies i write among you
and *for* you your champion my liver is strong my morals are stronger
so a native american woman will now accept this poem on my behalf
thus my sea rose is worth more than h.d.'s sea rose, she was not forthcoming
as to how she got hers. mine came from you, my love. i am forthcoming
i am the most important pest of my generation i will cut any man disagrees
into 198,000 pieces, i will starve him for 563 days i will make salt of his loins,
my stone wall frost's stone wall what is the difference really, i mean really.
i am younger and suppler than he was i can make it up the hill ruined farms
cellars and maple buckets rusted appreciate in years. so what. so go away. go
to uh, a vortex don't come out until you have sixteen foolhardy sexual plans
for the next four evenings. artillery practice artillery practice jeans commercial
i have been made brash like these things and i look good when doing my thing.

THE MATRONS

The books are stupid thin wives.
They glare from the shelves not
knowing what they want of me.
They glare from the shelves are
victims of my fingers, carelessly
caught in the action or otherwise
skippily skimming to the finish.
They glare from the shelves, out
and indicting. I can't but marvel
at the dozens of cocktails each'd
order. Each'd have a vanity plate
ballet, apple coulis'd. As it stands
they merely stand, idle coils idle
dolls, idle self idols compresséd
face to face back to back, pining
for room within which to preen.

CONCRETE POEM
[SONNET AVEC CHIENS]

What is the shape of a concrete poem aspiring toward formlessness?
What is my heft when I die and am stuffed into a little urn?
Will the ash ball up toward the bottom, like iced tea crystals
do at the bottom of a pitcher? And then the top will be all fluffy
like my favorite kitty cat cloudbank, the hooker about whom I dream?
I missed her comment about what love looks like after a mafia assassination
or perhaps she said that Tomas Tranströmer was a boring alpha male.
Love letters are scattered on the floors of many Arabs, Americans,
Frenchpeople, Canadians, and Africans. Who'd I forget? What pulped
will they look like? The letters, I mean? OK, and or the Arabs, Americans,
Frenchpeople, Canadians, and Africans? When a love letter is burned
does the beloved feel a celebratory twinge? Is death a movieset pencil
in the mind of a Surrealist? New Formalist? New York School dandy?
What good are cremains when the watch dogs stop sniffing them?

À LA PLAGE

Marie, Marie, wear your swimsuit free
of the glances of varíed perverts. Marie,

Marie, justify philosophy by spreading
your thighs to the throngs make them

believe. Marie, Marie, sliver up eternity
in a crystal goblet let me have a morsel.

Marie, Marie, your yellow breasts cap-
tivate me, orange-strípéd buttocks pick

the trunks from your crack do it slowly,
do it slightly, inconspicuous be. Marie,

Marie, French boys are the best for thee
I came via family from Quebec, Granby,

to be accurate. There's a zoo and take you
someday I will for popcorn and rides for

free. I've got a voucher. Marie, Marie, why
do you forsake me? Please, to take note: my

erection burns, won't back down, look at my
trousers. There up high, Marie, a windsock

& a windvane, even god's feeling the groove.
Mon cherie, god even is. Even god is, Marie.

DARK BALLAD OF THE 73RD PAGE

Sonnet avec filles.
Them: the old ones:
have they lived full lives
or are they near the end?
I never know how to feel
about that, when toward me
an old woman approaches
and I see the coffee cup's
trembling in her liverish
hand. One, the redhead,
must be seventy-five and
she works with machines.
I know not how she sees
their buttons, how she makes
this her world as she nears
its end. The last thing she's
very well capable of seeing's
a screen with pixeled words
strung like beads across a valley,
lain atop a ridge, to be followed
through forest by a young boy
and, upon reaching its end, will
he find a great fill-in-the-blank

we've all been after. This woman's
a ditch for my pity. For amiable
pity. I am sure once she cooked
for a husband, companion lesbian,
and it was fennel'd and good. Drink
your coffee you have earned it you
have earned nothing else but by your
having been here the right to die.

THIRTY-NINE THREADS [MORTALITÉ]

I.

Secret lucky hillock in the northwestern reaches of the White Mountain National Forest,
for somebody, at least I've not one but I've got a lucky pond tucked into a sad notch pocket

II.

Fixtures ceramic-wristed electric cords stapled to insulational plastic and rafters about 18″
apart in the rabbit coop man 2002 last time James Elmer Jackson shoveled a path reaching it

III.

Greek cookies in a jar in a cheap diner sans sesame seeds, Stravoula Ziakas Jackson still makes them with trembling hands goodness I shall
miss her more than mountains and that says a lot

IV.

Taking the boat out to the cusp of harbour and Atlantic brisk sunny July or so Maine childhood
weekend, Albert Hanninen master woodworker and fashioner of teak, voyaging uncle engineer

V.

Down to Boston MFA and Isabella Stewart Gardner and into Manchester NH and many many
books of art watercolour classes too Joanne Jackson Hanninen demure short brown hair, glasses

VI.

Father o father you will me a long white mane father nails and work gloves Richard Dennis Paquin this may be the first time I've long written
out your name Greetings let's have a chat

VII.

Mother your antiques all about you and funny anti-socialite reclusion were you ever on a hill and did your white dress blow in slow breeze Joy Jackson Paquin where do you train your eyes

VIII.

Nathan Paquin no middle name much tougher and more practical than most grip the knife and onion, precision dishes in winter apple orchards potato pumpkin patches don't stand a chance

IX.

Jill Jackson Skilling the rebel once but very mature I recall you cracked up a teenage car and gramp didn't flinch. You always bought the right records you hung a Terrapin Station poster

X.

I defy you to quantify into two lines of approximately thirty total words each major blood character in the stage-play production on-broadway of the only earthly appearance ballet

XI.

I defy myself to come to believe in god but you know I get more sensitive each year to stimuli
I swear each autumn on the trails the scent of brooks and leaves gets more seriously tinged

XII.

Do you feel this like you're running toward the horizon and have been doing it for years and finally upon reaching the hillock arrival x-marked zone nothing but an unsurprising boulder

XIII.

Not one photo exists of the entire group together. Cold ground to traipse

XIV.

The road is down the hill near the pine trunk former sentinel tree from which a rabbitry sign had dangled for decades. They would come for fur and meat now the squeak of icicle nothing

XV.

In some regions they work in coal mines all day and here she worked in the shoe shop got
rides home from best co-worker friends and now they are all dead I watched them dwindle

XVI.

I know not how she feels to have lost all earthly friends and to watch her beloved vanish in-
to the forest like a leg-shot fox wounded stumbling though dignified to its long-gone den

XVII.

And there somewhere out in the forest acreage is the den in the forest floor out in the woods
and I played there with my brother for years and never saw any place like it fern and clover

XVIII.

Cold circumvent an ocean's long journey to the tropical zone

XIX.

Bahámian hurricane drifting yacht and friends now-distant what was the deck like teak and still
as the world was any option you wanted for thousands of miles on any side of the little cabin

XX.

What is it like to see the stars everywhere for nights on end equatorial journey rum no doubt
how wild were you?, you're steady and studious enough to build tiny meticulous artifacts

XXI.

Matisse for the first time, tell me about it because then you ran with it for decades and painting
is something you never even once did. Thousands of canvases could you catalog your seeing

XXII.

I lash out with language stuck in a particular gear of angry diction.

XXIII.

This is not a unique condition parents reader everything will come there will be a final dinner a final hike final hill final horizon line a finish
line final handcrafted decoy in the workshop longs

XXIV.

longs for water it shall never touch. I project the inanimate object would longeth for water for
I am a Romantic and this is why people craft narratives about mortality and family I do believe

XXV.

believe in the wicked hinge wicked wind or something. Friends and children secure all stones
they are the truest material within and through them we can represent our universe order it

XXVI.

Language as material I was just getting to know Robert Creeley and then he died. I was just
trying to make a connection and god threw a cement block choke-hold on destiny on his head

XXVII.

head of musicks coming down the line I was just getting to know Richard Johnson pianist
and professor we were to lunch on downtown and then the spinets bent, luan scratched up

XXVIII.

Aerial balloon moss-covered skookumchuck katabatic slice climbed so many autumn rapids
to summits stared out at the foggiest comings-of-dusk I consider myself lucky to have seen

XXIX.

Je viens my daughters, *je viens* my son over here nevermind the hanging vine the sun through it bewitching doesn't begin to describe the
perils of the shores of love and of suffering and of hurt

XXX.

Je viens my wife, will you even wait for me but if you do make it classic, clutch with two hands by its wicker handle a simple colonial basket
within which quietly peach and apple fester

XXXI.

Valeria victrix plus one. Sonnet plus one equals exploded sonnet. Let us then quantify family's
several acres of forest which sometimes flood in spots known as sinkholes, skunkly and mealy

XXXII.

Ethan Paquin all my clothes are wet, sinkhole, far removal from the gulf from the top of Bond or Cannon on wedding-night's-eve, swore off
writing violently sucker-punched the act & now look

XXXIII.

now look at what has happened, another poet meditating on family and mortality and using, in
the title, English so's to dignify and elevate and separate from the pack his piece oh cleverness

XXXIV.

clever children, trick death by writing and painting, trick the mountains by eating magnets
trick the earth and the explorers and the sun, eat substantial metals for further fortification

XXXV.

Crossing a pine-plank bridge in a small fishing town in Prince Edward Island, I was struck
by the standard grade of road, mostly flat tending toward the cracked and it made me smile

XXXVI.

I rode a horse that summer, children Kelley did too she was pregnant smiling exhilirous
tiny belly not showing but there she was up and down against the gray sky slow motion

XXXVII.

The horses only aware of the gap between the trees, the corridor, and so they went, we atop
were mere and ancillary in some bizarre way—gesso showing through were it all a painting

XXXVIII.

Upon returning the owner and his wife thanked us and took our money (gently)

XXXIX.

and after the exchange the experience ended. And we kept going, don't remember where I'll let you know once I get there and may even
write a poem about it, or issue a report about it.

COMPOSITION EXPLOSION [TREELINE NARRATIVE]

sharp little pussy yes
indeed this's the time'f
day when forests do
empty of theirs in the
sea   of their myriad
clacks and mushrooms
of their benign fox-like
canopy-clipper fog-ins
acoasting down slopes
whishing   it all goes
disappears into the no-
man's-bay of darkness
tents in thousands ar-
rayed clock points or
dryads glowing faint
gainst purpling skies
and yesm we will kiss
you've not got hair but
that which I project
from out the miracle-
dream cesspool swim-
ming toward a cove's

the act of sound of river

behind us below us is

what valley is   let me arrange us in a compositional field river there,

mountain there, mountain two there, ridgeline there, purple clouds there, shadowy fog skims as such, your hair blowing that way, a few tents

    likely down there, I'm on this here you're across close to me, probably mushrooms nearby birch clusters   over there (? —

who can say in which direction is ocean is Saturn is surrealism)

who can say how you're an answer for me mere complication but you're smart so let's talk until the looks like mallow shoot from birds' eyes.

    Forest scene, artist unknown.

INSUFFICIENCY

The process of this here book: needless war's still
roiling akettle, I've been masturbating too much,
I've not been having enough Lax, the kettle's broken
got caked with room-bile dust, shifting foundation's
cracked a jamb, you are the brownest-haired pain-
in-the-ass on earth and have yet to acknowledge me.

Skimming the photo albums for my favorite artists,
directors, musicians and painters to see their stares
at age 38—that's me. Is something in them in us all
like the way skin looks/sags/is lighted, the way hair
gets wild in particular ways? Is work accomplished
at this age particularly dignified? Desert nightstand.

Deer reflect in puddles ripple in air monument gray
loom in the background which is still all one plane
in a small pool of sidewalk or asphalt water. Chime
and star are no different, advertisements for inchoate
ephemerality. My ever-graying head, never stopped
biting my nails. Tobogganing near the apartments,

repainted green every other year. V-band of crows
in November, this is language bequeathéd us. Books

of tick-mark oil change dentist tire inflations, medals
from county fairs lops and New Zealands placed won
a few times. Where are we going. Can you teach me
teach me to lay beneath the stars in a hay field simply

like the characters in dignified and truly sad artworks
from America's pastoral age. I know I never want this
busyness, this wheat-as-commodity, the Eakins scull-
race as up-to-the-minute sports news entertainment,
the naked male body as object of right-wing hatred,
town-common church house as more than pretty site,

a mother as political operative, students as suspicious
lanterns avoiding the match, I never wanted clouds
tin wood chips to be overlooked suffering music where
is it now? Deer and puddles I don my boots to reach
you. The process of this book is like a hike's process
I stop for water, kneel, see ranges painted stray blue

nothing so funereal so to commemorate I give to thee
an ending couplet look at all the white beneath it

LUMPEN DISTRICT

A wreath for thee. Blister
a water for thee, a writhe
for me my aching side's
got me, burden burden
burden in the icy lands.

Broke down here white
space all around & dead
rye's not helicopter'd by
west winds as in summer
rather it's matted by pain

hugs the earth barnyard
clumps and mud violent
in season. We're huddling
twisting wreaths in snow.
Black boot-tops contrast

with brown rye with white
space everywhere else. Not
even tree green or sky blur.
The hurt is all around here's
our only organ it's broken.

SPRING EX MACHINAE

Paper weight idling drab-a-drab March and April
(I mean, sullen skies as heavy as a paperweight or
silk streaming floes and airs and snows of whites
very light, weighing less than paper, which itself's
usually as white as now's wind and crush of cold
afternoon's post-clock-forward cloud filtration) I
hate everything for which you two bastards stand

Sun's no greek-orange rivulet streaming through
now the curtains hung here days are but chain link
in stature, are needlepoint suicide notes, are upward-
ratcheted dramamine pre-worm-and-wisteria-thaw
potemkin settlements The queen of internal optimism
passes waving from the deck all seems bright enough
well how simple and stupid this woman can often be.

MY EVANGELISM
[OH DATE OF EXPIRY]

oh date of expiry,
my children's silhouettes atop a four-thousand-foot peak, perhaps on Moosilauke perhaps on Kinsman perhaps on Tripyramid,

oh date of expiry,
my letters sealed in wax paper February here and brooding, pepper me geranial sun blank with some species of damn feeling,

oh date of expiry,
Toward an art that means is where we're all headed, right?, is what the programme said was the name of the new exhibition,

oh exhibition,
got to get my work hung in there else what of me will remain oh comes that day of expiry, it comes and comes like inkburst birds,

oh date of expiry,
my children silhouetted atop the high New Hampshire mountain and from medium-long they summit graze for best vantage,

oh date of expiry,
my letters to a woman I was once inside but whose eyes escape me, how does that exactly occur, once the only pears for harvest,

oh date of expiry,
toward memento mori toward death mask and impale, moon face gravelly mortgage levied I keep marching though I don't see fit,

oh fit, sturdy field
how often I raged through you on my way, on my way out on my way beyond, and humbly I return and beseech you my re-entry,

oh date of expiry,

there are bone plots in this field and many of them, this's a mile long rectangular field and all I love will be abandoned out of sight,

oh date of expiry,

my children picking blueberries on a warm trailside August brook echoes deep below but a benevolent farness not breakneck chasm,

oh date of expiry,

my letters bound in a leather strap neither it nor the letters exist, I never got it down anywhere for the pencil's irreliant,

oh pencil, break-

neck pencil it's not your fault the greens aren't as green as you say. Surrealism's not your fault seaside jottings on red sunsets' glory,

oh date of expiry,

one last breath nothing beyond but the final one now that is difficult to conceive, look the cows are being weaned smells like wheat

oh date of expiry,

sounds of boats shuttling and humans having fun on the decks, here I am in my imagination near a channel root canal vibrant,

oh date of expiry,

my children coming down the trail bushels and boots the odd kicked-up rock sounds of jays composition in mute green and yellow,

oh colours,

it is your birthday and our anniversary. I first used you several decades ago and then I learned what your names were but what's more,

oh date of expiry,

I refuse to stop learning when I am not. I will accrete. For all intents a mountain's dead but children are vibrant and blueberries too

Children upon it are vibrantly skipping down its trail
blueberries hopping from their baskets
and they don't mind and the mountain neither

and somewhere in the mountain I will lodge
myself, will refuse to be sentried nor
will I be tried. Crows keep skimming above I will never stop paying attention to you.

UNRELIABLE NARRATIVE

I don't like the rain because
tomorrow it's going to rain.

I don't like tomorrow because
tomorrow it's going to rain.

I don't like me because I know
tomorrow it's going to rain.

I launched all-out war based
on the lies told in this poem.

LINGUAE

Image: precise snow, shard
enough to thread the O in O,
the minute triangle of A, the
soft pregnancy of d.   Image:
its flit downward brick mill
grain elevator approaching
and toxic blast zone of, say,
a city like Buffalo. Images:
arrays of shards of snow pre-
empted from descent, front
arctic & thick sheet flapping
and laundry hanging snow
just stuck up there, heaven-
wards or whatever, to never
arrive. To never but billow.

NEIGE [THREE SCENES]

1.

aimless animal-coloured tumbler your library's aphotically indeterminate
you morning the ground to groggier-than-usual's millions of earmarks;
there are no students eternal only stop signs to bark commands rufescent,
only stalléd cirri shelves and shelves of them bustling ether of nowhere
only my eyes no millions of other watchers imprecise tumbler heft spills
from the seat of god onto our laps a necklace to be untangled with bones
and a half-erased script and stumps for motivations, ut pictura cirrus this's
all that comes to mind Latin for curl of hair thus the portrait of a girl who's
blanched perhaps she's suffered, perhaps she's been spooked, likely in love

2.

in love and staring out a window ut drizzle poesis, so goeth poetry as drizzle,
lovers' crazy ideas of where their object went the evening before, before snow
tumbled before her eyes saw the result of the katabatic front. Ut drizzle poesis,
long gray nuance between stanzas the meander from cup of tea to the next one,
snow's meanwhile abstraction an easy metaphor for the week. Young woman
in love as you are please, do not comb your hair—I see you motion for a brush
through the window I watch and clasp myself, do not to the narrative of dawn
surrender, stay wild and pained and look that way. This is not mere entertain-
ment. Snow tumbles aimless, accretes aphotic my gaze though is fixed upon you

3.

such sentimental passages about love, weather and fixéd male gazes hunter
as he is, supposedly, of erotic experience wherever to be found. I'm stupid
like dander, or clover. I transcend no fence reach no apple bough. Limitless
are other poetries of the engines, of the random, of the idiomatic, of the pop-
unders and overt flâneurist grit-amenities. I wear a poem like this like, say,
a dead braid or a last match, bit of its tip scratched off, the thing useless for
cigarette to say nothing of survival or bonfire at the beach where the talk's
of sex and nothing but sex. A deadened band of cirrus is known to haunt us
at our windows the girl and I like snapped taper candles, outside the snows

ZEN

She was on a hill doing pichagis.
I would rather her aphonic but
she said she can't: harmony is
one noisy business, apparently.

She leapt I watcht the interplay
of arriving dusk, kicking legs,
and trees. The scene was a snow-
globe unshook, a no-intertitled

foreign non-linear movie. It all
was life and it all made no sense
but it was big like frigate orange
like the slow shadow of sunset.

SYLVAN HISTORY

Camera got my grandfather in it—summery date-stamped
August stroll with my tiny daughter. Just one still. Cupola's

top left, weathervane obscured by backgrounded pines, sky
muted, can't tell whether it was really gray or blue, he's got

on his trademark bunnet and a short-sleeved brown shirt,
gray khakis a little hiked-up. Up the cart path he walks,

heading right, turning a corner, almost off the picture and
into a grove hinted-at by a branch of maple that juts out.

Sunflowers through a workshop window, composition's
middle and off to the left, can be seen. Only stark colors

in the entire photo, and just a clip of them. This taste is
all there is left. He's in a bed in another state and dying

and though his back's turned to us one can tell he walks
both knowing the walk's nearly over, cart path to front

door nearly crested, and defying it. His left hand's not
merely holding my daughter's, one can see it guiding

nearly pulling her fresh legs filly up a strange incline.
I'm going to show you a place he giddily expresses or

seems to *but whereas I'll forever from the frame from
the photograph disappear, you'll know your duty walk*

*and love the walk, past the maples atop dew-cool grass
and near the sunflowers* which at any rate will endure.

DESPAIR THAT IS COGNIZANT OF BEING DESPAIR

". . . continue to work out your salvation with fear and trembling."
PHILIPPIANS 2:12

Found we have found no murals of god on saturn that's
how we know there is in fact no god oh I know it hurts

greening meadow of malice's aforethoughts of eden of
buckshoots careening loose-tooth of ghetto and chaff

celestialene milk-run people're being cast out what's
the big deal, it's the all-out holes dug in the sand pits

roadside blast proliferatio can not perceive mother no
more codeine taxi services now hit all the right notes

scansion cuspal black and white distal poetry the dentist
page the office anger's appointment world some abscess

RAIN [THREE SCENES]

I.

preference rain communion
I can bestow through fogs
and barriers come the sea
where kite I will guide you
through fens avow brackish
lingering pools, all the shells
for you are you I deem this

II.

frigate proliferation thumb's
cold widowwatch agonizery
and beach and dead herring
nets fray words of the day
is barrier young boy leans
knows what he sees waves
mother and future in ocean

III.

half-sonnet texture a rain-
still and stand here a loupe
for the stills to study wash
and backlash tidal or dorsal
vélar plosive caskets crawl
grenade gutter grab o drab
impending cum of stratus

STASIS SHOT IN B/W ALTHOUGH COLOUR WAS AVAILABLE

Jeezum crow, I need to get down and off
this typewriter. Y'know the ilk of a Montana star,
I need something like a Montana star's flit over a burg
like Montana. Nightly my tent is sexless-pitched angled in
a ditch off the refinery road. I need something in a woman's
never been seen a quilt handed to me on a gripping coastline
or a safety pin chrysolith for to quick-patch my weak moments
into one bundle so as to make the journey from point to point on
the line segment known as aethereal professional-cultural Buffalo.
I need something like return and revolve the mnbvcxzlkjhgfdsa-
poiuytrewq something overt all the time but innate and novel
like going backwards on typewriter keys. I need take notes
for next time around here's a chute there a chasm here
a chute there a chasm around has got to be a fence
upon which to lean and survey. Skyscape check
directions check directionless check and I
check check the watch, in, write thé, off,
mate and the box. Tiny tiny square.

EXEUNT

Let me not tell you a story, I already did
Ghetto and Calf, 1962
Landfall traffic jam
The actors are confusedly ready to be freed
A director huffs his monocle clean
Surprise of Sunrise, 1965,
primitive pastel found in an attic
The props and scenery
The medium-close
Tons of concepts: how to enact
Crying Clown, 1974
a dentist's office hijack
and kidnap lee shore
a calm hatred of oneself
and one's refusal to, upon being joined with one,
eleven. Sylvan death I await you til I rot
I give thee mine anger in Chinese food
buckets the white ones all cheap
with white and tin handle flim.
Burned Skyscraper, 1925
Let us all tell each other stories let us all
rule, let us all rule each other and
the stories of the other, govern

let us govern. Medium-Range Fireball, 2005
installation fuck-you fingerprint assessor
go home, the country road lemonade
housewife clothesline suicide made
curious the documentarian
Ella Fitzwatter, 2011
self-portrait in chromium filings
and glue, rabbit fur and family circi
Ashberian cocci narrative strands, I can't help
but be inspired and frustrated by so many
ouncing praetors. File cabinet hang-up
search every folder for the specs
and the stanzas. Landscape With Reclining Nude Terrorist 2006
we're so afraid and I just hate that. Let's take up arms
against idiots who hate art, who don't know art at all.
I renounce them standing against me folded arms
or clasped, I have defeated you via rejection.
I hate those who hate life,
who resign and recline
in a posited field of gold and honey and booty
on some posited green green hill. Traipsers.
I hate having and taking, I hate caged bird
metaphors hailed as brilliant, they're not
I hate multimillion mousepads and pen caps
bottle snaps and tooth cracks whip cream
sex trade aphid raid midnight sweat belt
buckle get me a beer bitch go to church

or die in flame Baptist haircut chap-lip
fuck-up cutthroat salvation macaroni
gramaphone dance party belly chain
virtue of slut gone ka-put democracy
string-em-by-the-balls Georgia Alabama
backwaters heavy water Niagara Frontier
atomic toothpaste cable modem overflow
pock-mark flow chart post-O'Hara traipse
and forty-dollar steak poetry fundraise
for eternity fuel the machine elected
tiny tiny square decisions limits
cloud versus cloud sad's an overlap
quiet interplay Hurricane and Smile 1975
stark godwhite and ubergray frown
love in the form of missionary
unrequited, hellfire bouquet
cloud from cloud, outro
sift and waft caught
on the hill cloud's
mirage no promise
fruit of desert opent
for divorce business's
multimillion degrees traversd
when it all goes down and ends, if.
Flamethrower and Apples, 1892.
Man With Grandson, 1377.
Bridge Over Troubled Spring Water Bottles, 2002.

Self-Portrait With Exit Wound, 1641.

Scurrying Hares, 1590.

Hidden Cameras Are Watching, 1966.

Fargo, North Dakota, 1980.

Liminal Nexus, 1952.

Tree Split By Lightning, 1981.

Spilled Milk and Mop, 1977.

Patron Saint of Gunpowder, 2012.

Millionth Self-Reflexive Artwork, 1972.

Monolith, 1823.

Glory to the Newborn King, 020.

Vomit in aisle twenty.

We can take you at register twenty.

Check out the poet's register in line twenty.

Revisit the posts on page twenty.

Mile-marker twenty.

Random lottery-ball twenty.

Milk-money twenty furlongs

left, break down and we'll shoot.

For your own good. Keep straight

ahead, sparkling forest, go issue a report.

Find a spring drink from it and come

back, tell us about its heavenly taste

and its innocent trickling.

NOTES

ENDEARMENT

Sonnet: the structure was inspired by a Matt Hart poem of the same name.

Non-Linear Pastoral Depressive: inspired by the Homer painting "A Temperance Meeting," also known as "Noon Time" or "Gloucester Farm."

Life Imitates Cento: borrows lines from Neil Young's "Cinnamon Girl."

Endearment II.4: "Distance: versts" is from Marina Tsvetaeva's "To Boris Pasternak."

PATRON SAINT GUNPOWDER

Kinoglaz: "Our eyes see very little and very badly—so people dreamed up the microscope to let them see invisible phenomena; they invented the telescope . . . now they have perfected the cine- camera to penetrate more deeply into the visible world." Vertov, 1926. Glass-eye: deep peering, beyond-perception of what's there beneath there.

Subnarrative of Nantucket: thinking of WCW's poem.

Disjunctive Field [Artillery]: cf. *Aguirre, der Zorn Gottes* by Herzog, who is also elsewhere (*Winter Country Lot; After Truth; Three Threads*).

Lumpen District: thinking of Eisenstein's *Stachka* and The Band's "Hobo Jungle."

Neige [Three Scenes]: "beach where the talk's / of sex and nothing but sex" inspired by/owes to a line from Ronald Palmer's poem "Logic of Celibacy" (from *Logicalogics*).

Despair That is Cognizant of Being Despair: title after Kierkegaard.

ABOUT THE AUTHOR

ETHAN PAQUIN is the author of four other books of poems including *The Violence,* released by Ahsahta Press in 2005. He is the founding editor of the longstanding online literary journal *Slope*, and is co-founder and director of the nonprofit small poetry press, Slope Editions. He lives and teaches in his native New Hampshire.

AHSAHTA PRESS

SAWTOOTH POETRY PRIZE SERIES

2002: Aaron McCollough, *Welkin* (Brenda Hillman, judge)

2003: Graham Foust, *Leave the Room to Itself* (Joe Wenderoth, judge)

2004: Noah Eli Gordon, *The Area of Sound Called the Subtone* (Claudia Rankine, judge)

2005: Karla Kelsey, *Knowledge, Forms, The Aviary* (Carolyn Forché, judge)

2006: Paige Ackerson-Kiely, *In No One's Land* (D. A. Powell, judge)

2007: Rusty Morrison, *the true keeps calm biding its story* (Peter Gizzi, judge)

2008: Barbara Maloutas, *the whole Marie* (C. D. Wright, judge)

2009: Julie Carr, *100 Notes on Violence* (Rae Armantrout, judge)

2010: James Meetze, *Dayglo* (Terrance Hayes, judge)

2011: Karen Rigby, *Chinoiserie* (Paul Hoover, judge)

2012: T. Zachary Cotler, *Sonnets to the Humans* (Heather McHugh, judge)

NEW SERIES

1. Lance Phillips, *Corpus Socius*
2. Heather Sellers, *Drinking Girls and Their Dresses*
3. Lisa Fishman, *Dear, Read*
4. Peggy Hamilton, *Forbidden City*
5. Dan Beachy-Quick, *Spell*
6. Liz Waldner, *Saving the Appearances*
7. Charles O. Hartman, *Island*
8. Lance Phillips, *Cur aliquid vidi*
9. Sandra Miller, *oriflamme.*
10. Brigitte Byrd, *Fence Above the Sea*
11. Ethan Paquin, *The Violence*
12. Ed Allen, *67 Mixed Messages*
13. Brian Henry, *Quarantine*
14. Kate Greenstreet, *case sensitive*
15. Aaron McCollough, *Little Ease*
16. Susan Tichy, *Bone Pagoda*
17. Susan Briante, *Pioneers in the Study of Motion*
18. Lisa Fishman, *The Happiness Experiment*

AHSAHTA PRESS

This book is set in Apollo MT type with Eurostile titles
by Ahsahta Press at Boise State University.
Cover design by Quemadura / Book design by Janet Holmes
Printed in Canada.

AHSAHTA PRESS

2013

JANET HOLMES, DIRECTOR

CHRISTOPHER CARUSO

JODI CHILSON

KYLE CRAWFORD

CHARLES GABEL

JESSICA HAMBLETON, *intern*

RYAN HOLMAN

MELISSA HUGHES, *intern*

TORIN JENSEN

ANNIE KNOWLES

STEPHA PETERS

JULIE STRAND